W9-CDO-179

By Barbara Allman

Lerner Publications Company
Minneapolis

For Grandpa Tony, who taught me about money but gave me true riches.

Lerner Publications Company
A division of Lerner Publishing Group
241 First Avenue North
Minneapolis, MN 55401 U.S.A.

Website address: www.lernerbooks.com

Library of Congress Cataloging-in-Publication Data

Allman, Barbara.
Banking / by Barbara Allman.
p. cm. — (How economics works)
Includes bibliographical references and index.
ISBN-13: 978-0-8225-2148-8 (lib. bdg. : alk. paper)
ISBN-10: 0-8225-2148-2 (lib. bdg. : alk. paper)
1. Banks and banking—Juvenile literature. I. Title. II. Series.
HG1609.A45 2006
332.1—dc22 2004019711

Manufactured in the United States of America
1 2 3 4 5 6 – DP – 11 10 09 08 07 06

Table of Contents

CHAPTER 1
U.S. BANKING— WHAT'S THE STORY?

Imagine yourself in the 1600s, walking along a street in a town during the early days of colonial America. You pass a few shops, a school, and a church. What's missing? A bank! There were no banks in the early American colonies.

Before the United States was born, Britain ruled the American colonies. American colonists used British coins to pay for things. Settlers from England brought these coins with them to America. But there just weren't

Wampum beads threaded together into lengths of set amounts, such as the belt above, often served as currency in colonial times.

enough to go around. Sometimes the colonists traded tobacco or Native American wampum (beads) for the goods they needed. They also used Spanish coins. The silver Spanish coins, called reals, were soft. They could be cut into eight bits to make change. So these coins were sometimes called "pieces of eight." In 1652 the Massachusetts Bay Colony began making its own coins. But England ruled Massachusetts and wanted to keep control over the money there. In 1686 England ordered Massachusetts to stop making coins.

BANK ON IT During colonial times, Massachusetts paid its soldiers with promissory notes. A promissory note was written on paper. It promised to pay a certain amount of money to the person who held the paper. This was the first paper money used in America.

LAND BANKS

The colonists wanted a better system, so they began to set up land banks. These banks were started by groups of farmers and store owners. Land banks helped farms and businesses by lending them money. A land bank issued, or gave out, its own paper money.

The British didn't want the Americans to make their own money. The British thought that might take away some of the power the British king had over America. In 1751 the British rulers passed a law. It said that no new land banks could be created, and no paper money could be used in the colonies. The colonists soon got fed up with British laws, and in 1775 they rebelled. The American colonists won their war for independence in 1783, and the United States was born. Americans were free to decide their own laws, including banking laws.

A CENTRAL BANK

Alexander Hamilton was the first secretary of the treasury for the new United States of America. The secretary of the treasury advises the president on money matters and reports to Congress on the nation's money situation. Hamilton wanted to set up a central, or federal, bank that would manage the country's money. But Secretary of State Thomas Jefferson thought that plan would give the federal government too much power. He wanted the individual states to control their own banks and money.

In 1791 the U.S. Congress did create a central bank—the First Bank of the United States. It operated for twenty years.

VALUE ADDED

During the Free Banking Era, banks could choose designs for their bank notes from an engraver's sample book. The American Bank Note Company offered designs of battles, famous patriots and scientists, flowers, and even popular celebrities.

But Americans couldn't agree whether a central bank was a good idea. Sometimes the nation had a central bank, and sometimes it didn't. The Second Bank of the United States began in 1816 and lasted until 1836.

Then things got colorful. The Free Banking Era (1836–1866) began. State laws allowed states, cities, counties, railroads, stores, and individuals to open their own banks. These banks issued their own notes (printed their own money). All the banks chose their own colors and designs, so many different kinds of bank notes existed. Money from a Virginia bank looked different from that of a Michigan bank. Citizens in one state didn't always recognize the money from another state. This made it very easy for criminals, called counterfeiters, to make fake money. Therefore, many citizens didn't trust paper money.

MONEY TALK The Bank of Michigan printed notes with a wild panther on them. They were nicknamed wildcat notes. When the notes lost their value, bank depositors lost too. Soon people called any failed business deal a "wildcat deal."

The banks kept gold and silver in reserve. If they wanted to, people could exchange their paper money for gold or silver coins at the bank. But some bankers were dishonest. They didn't have enough gold or silver on hand to exchange for the bank notes. This made

Wildcats

As the country got bigger in the middle 1800s, the number of state banks grew. Problems also grew. Some banks were called "wildcat banks" because they were founded in faraway places. It was said that wildcats could reach these banks more easily than people. That would make it hard for people to exchange a bank's notes for gold or silver coins. If a bank's notes became worthless, they were called "broken" and the bank "went broke."

the paper money worthless. Without a central bank, the system was a jumble again.

In 1861 President Abraham Lincoln named Salmon P. Chase as secretary of the treasury. Chase is called the father of the U.S. banking system because he wrote the National Banking Act of 1863. This law set up a system of national banks. Banks that were part of the national banking system issued the same bank notes. The new national bank notes were carefully controlled by the U.S. government.

The national banks issued paper money called greenbacks. Greenbacks were national bank notes printed with green ink on one side. In 1865 another law taxed state bank notes. At that point, many state banks joined the national system to avoid paying the tax. All the different banks finally began to issue the same paper money.

MONEY Makers In the 1860s, Salmon P. Chase had his own picture printed on the U.S. one-dollar bill and President Abraham Lincoln's on the five. Since more one-dollar bills were used, some people thought he was trying to become more popular than Lincoln.

Calling Out the Reserves

Even with a national banking system, banks still had many ups and downs. Sometimes people panicked and tried to take all their deposits (money) out of banks. When this happened, banks ran out of money and had to close. Many people lost all their savings in these "bank panics."

MONEY TALK *Deposit* is a word that comes from Latin, the language of the ancient Romans. In Latin, *de* means "away" and *positus* means "placed." When you deposit money, you place it away.

To prevent more bank panics, Congress passed the Federal Reserve Act in 1913. To make sure that no single bank had too much power, Congress divided the nation into twelve districts, or regions. Each district had its own reserve bank, or central bank, for that part of the country. Each central bank kept reserves (gold and silver to back up the money) for the banks in its region.

The Federal Reserve made the banking system more stable for a while. Then, in 1929, things took a turn for the worse. To make more money, many banks used the money people deposited to purchase stock in private companies. When the stocks went up in value, banks made a profit. But if the value of the stocks went down, banks lost money. On October 29, 1929, the stock market crashed—the value of stocks went way down. Many banks lost a lot of money, including their reserves. Citizens began to worry that their money

What Is Stock?

Companies issue stock certificates to borrow money. People and organizations that buy the stock are buying a part of the company. They hope to make money by buying stocks at one price and cashing them in for a higher price later. The stock market is the industry that buys and sells stocks.

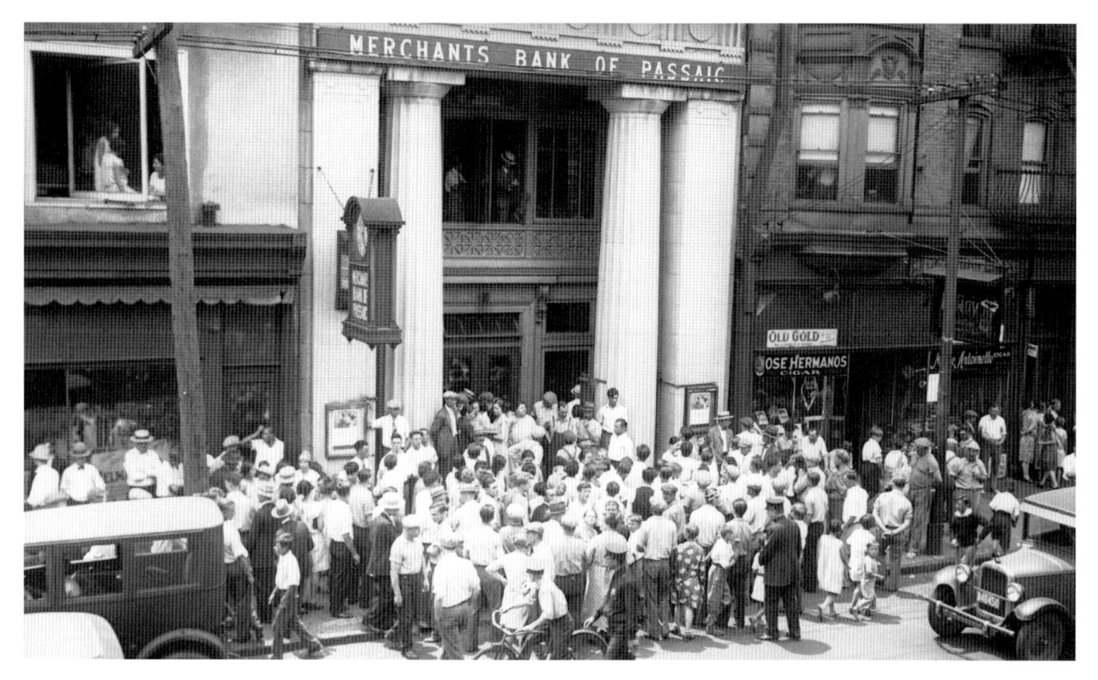

A mob of concerned depositors gathers outside the Merchants Bank in Passaic, New Jersey, after the 1929 stock market crash.

was not safe in the banks, so they raced to withdraw their money. But many banks had run out of money. Time and time again, banks failed, and people lost their deposits. This period of economic hardship was called the Great Depression (1929–1941). President Franklin D. Roosevelt knew something had to be done. He had to give people a reason to trust the banks. On March 6, 1933, he closed all banks for four days, calling it a "bank holiday." Only safe, strong banks were allowed to open again.

To rebuild people's trust in banks, Congress passed the Banking Act of 1933. It set up a government insurance agency, the Federal Deposit Insurance Corporation, or FDIC. The agency guarantees that people will not lose their bank deposits.

Brother, Can You Spare a Dime?

The Great Depression (1929–1941) began in the United States on October 29, 1929, when the stock market crashed. Between 1930 and 1933, almost ten thousand U.S. banks failed. Businesses closed, and millions of people lost their jobs. Those who were lucky enough to have jobs saw their wages go down. People stood in long lines, called breadlines, to get handouts of food. Some begged for spare change on the streets.

Banks pay the FDIC for this insurance. Since the start of FDIC insurance, not a penny of insured deposits has been lost. The FDIC still insures bank deposits up to $100,000.

New Laws Protect People

In 1968 Congress passed the Truth in Lending Act. This law requires banks to treat people with honesty when lending them money. Banks must tell customers how much a loan would cost them in interest each year.

Before 1974 banks could decide whether to loan people money based on whether they were married or single, male or female. For example, a married woman might have been refused a loan without her husband's permission. The Equal Credit Opportunity Act of 1974 made it illegal for banks to discriminate against people because of their sex or living situation. In 1976 the law was changed to forbid discrimination by race, color, religion, country of birth, or age as well.

Chapter 2
Bank on It!

A bank is a business. People, other businesses, and even the government can deposit money in banks. Besides being a safe place for depositing money, banks also offer other money services.

When you make a deposit in a bank, the money doesn't just sit there. The bank uses it. While your money is in the bank, that money can earn interest, which means it can make more money. Interest is a fee paid for the use of money. When the bank uses the money you deposited, it pays you for the use of that money.

ANOTHER KIND OF BANK

People have been saving money for ages. About a thousand years ago in Britain, some people saved their money in clay pots called *pyggs*. Then one day, a potter had the bright idea to make a pygg that looked like a pig, and the piggy bank was born!

HOW DOES A BANK USE YOUR MONEY?

The bank uses your deposit to make more money. How does it do that? One way is by making loans. A loan allows someone to borrow money with a promise to pay it back within a certain amount of time. People might borrow money to buy something expensive, such as a car or a house. When borrowers pay back a loan, they also pay an extra charge to the bank. The extra charge is called interest. When you use the bank's money, you pay interest to the bank. Charging interest for loans is one way that banks make money.

SORTING OUT DIFFERENT KINDS OF FINANCIAL INSTITUTIONS

Commercial banks, savings and loan associations, mutual savings banks, and credit unions are all places where people can deposit money. Commercial banks provide all kinds of money services. They offer checking accounts, loans, and investment services. Investment services include such things as savings accounts, business investments, and real estate.

Savings and loan associations (S&Ls), mutual savings banks, and credit unions are sometimes called thrifts. They started up in the days when banks served mostly businesses and wealthy people. Banks didn't want to serve working-class people. The thrifts made saving more available to working people.

MONEY TALK *Thrifty* means being careful in spending. A thrifty shopper, for example, might look in more than one store and online to find the best price for a new CD.

Savings and loan associations used to be known as building and loan associations or homestead associations. Working people formed S&Ls to help each other buy homes. In 1831 a group of neighbors in Frankford, Pennsylvania, founded the Oxford Provident Building Association. It was the first savings and loan association in the United States. Members deposited their savings, and the association used the deposits to make home loans to its members. Savings and loan associations still make home loans.

Mutual savings banks benefit the people who deposit their savings there. The word *mutual* means "shared," or "joint." Mutual savings banks were first established in the early 1800s in Philadelphia, Pennsylvania, and Boston, Massachusetts. Working people wanted a way to save money for the future. Mutual savings banks were set up so depositors, rather than the bank owners, earned a profit. In modern times, mutual savings banks are

MONEY TALK Profit: the money left over after expenses are paid.

found mostly in the northeastern United States. They make home loans and offer savings and checking accounts.

Credit unions are another type of financial institution. They are usually formed by a group of people who do the same type of work. For example, members of a teachers' credit union work in schools. Credit unions are like a club. They offer many of the same services that commercial banks do but only to their own members. Some credit unions charge less interest than banks do for making similar loans. Members' savings may earn more interest than they would in a bank too.

FEDERAL RESERVE BANKS

The Federal Reserve System is sometimes called the Fed for short. You already know that the United States has twelve Federal Reserve banks. These are bankers' banks. You cannot go to a Federal Reserve bank and take out a loan. But other banks can.

VALUE ADDED

The Fed supplies banks with paper money and coins. But the Fed doesn't actually make new paper money (called Federal Reserve notes). The Bureau of Engraving and Printing, a part of the U.S. Treasury Department, prints new paper money. The U.S. Mint makes all U.S. coins.

MAP MATCHUP

The United States has twelve Federal Reserve banks. Using the map below, you can label each bank's location.

1. Boston, Massachusetts
2. New York, New York
3. Philadelphia, Pennsylvania
4. Cleveland, Ohio
5. Richmond, Virginia
6. Atlanta, Georgia
7. Chicago, Illinois
8. Saint Louis, Missouri
9. Minneapolis, Minnesota
10. Kansas City, Missouri
11. Dallas, Texas
12. San Francisco, California

One of the Fed's important jobs is checking on the way banks do their business. The Fed looks carefully at bank records and makes sure banks follow banking laws. It also influences the supply of money (the amount of money circulating in the country). The Fed gets paper money from the Bureau of Engraving and Printing (located in Washington, D.C.) and coins from the U.S. Mint. (Mints are located in Denver, Colorado; Philadelphia, Pennsylvania; San Francisco, California; and West Point, New York.) Banks and other financial institutions can then order coins and paper money from the Federal Reserve bank in their region. Banks deposit some of their reserves at the Fed too. The Fed sorts and counts the money and inspects it for counterfeits.

A Federal Reserve bank also clears checks and electronic transfers for the banks in its regions. When Ann writes a check to pay for groceries, the store deposits her check in its bank. The bank sends the check to the Fed. It makes sure Ann's bank has enough reserves to back her check. The Fed transfers that amount to the grocer's bank. Then the Fed sends Ann's check back to the bank it came from. High-speed machines at each Federal Reserve bank sort about a million checks each day. The machines also keep track of the amount of money to be added to or subtracted from each bank's reserves. That way the Federal Reserve bank can keep track of all the banks in its region.

Chapter 3
To Save or to Spend— That Is the Question

Lee and April decided to earn some money one summer. They used a computer to make a flyer. On it they listed yard work and pet care jobs they could do. Then they handed out the flyers in their neighborhood. If you are like Lee and April, you like to earn money too. Once you earn it, you have to decide what to do with it. You could spend all your money on small things. Or you might want to save it to buy something more expensive. Or you might choose to spend some and save some.

You could save your money in a piggy bank or in a shoebox under the bed. But then you might be tempted to spend it. Or your pet mouse might chew it up.

The safest place for your money is in a bank. Banks keep money in a locked vault. A vault is made of steel, and it's fireproof. A bank will guarantee that your money will be there when you want it. That's not all though. In a bank, your money goes to work, earning even more money for you.

That's Italian!

Modern banking began in Italy in the 1400s. Our English word *bank* comes from the Italian word *banca.* Hundreds of years ago in Italy, bankers did business from benches in the streets. The Italian word for bench is banca. If you wanted to see a man about some money matters in fifteenth-century Italy, you would go to a banca.

A Savings Account Works for You

When you keep your money in a savings account, the bank pays you interest. Let's say that you receive $100 in cash on your birthday. First, you write thank-you notes. Then you deposit the $100 in a bank. The bank agrees to pay you 5 percent interest every year. If you leave the money there for one year, you'll have $105. Happy birthday from your bank!

Dollars & Sense "A rich man is nothing but a poor man with money."
—W. C. Fields (1879–1946), a motion picture comedian

You can choose from two basic kinds of savings accounts. One is a passbook account, and the other is a statement account. More and more, banks offer an account that has both a passbook and a statement.

With a passbook account, the bank gives you a small booklet called a passbook. Each time you go to the bank, the bank teller records your deposits, withdrawals, and the interest you earn in the passbook. The passbook tells you the balance in your account. The balance is the amount of money left in your account. You can also make deposits at an automatic teller machine (ATM). (See Chapter 5 for more about ATMs.)

With a statement account, the bank sends you a printed

Words to Know

Withdraw means "to take out." When you make a withdrawal from your account, you take money out.

A teller is a person who counts. With the help of a computer, a bank teller counts money when taking it in and giving it out.

A bank statement is a printed report that states all the deposits, withdrawals, and any interest earned in your account each month.

record of your account every month. The statement shows how much money you have deposited, how much you have withdrawn, or taken out of your account, and how much interest you have earned that month. It also tells you the balance in your account.

Sign Me Up!

When you are ready to open a savings account, a parent can help you sign up for one at a bank. You will need to tell the person at the bank your name, address, date of birth, and Social Security number. That person can show you how to fill out a form to deposit or withdraw your money. These forms are called deposit slips and withdrawal slips.

Social Security Administration

If you were born in the United States, you probably have a Social Security number. Your parents probably signed you up with the Social Security Administration when you were born. They received your Social Security card with your Social Security number on it. Your parents report the Social Security numbers of everyone in your family when they pay their income tax each year.

You will need a Social Security number when you are old enough to get a job (or open a bank account). Social Security is a government program for workers. When you get a job, part of each paycheck is deposited into the Social Security program. The government uses your Social Security number to keep track of the payments you make. Social Security helps retired workers (those who have stopped working), disabled workers, and their families. If you retire, become disabled, or die, you or your family members will receive payments from the Social Security program.

Some savings accounts require a minimum balance. This means you need to keep a certain amount of money in the account. If the balance falls below that amount, the bank can collect a monthly charge. One good thing about being a kid is that the bank probably won't require a minimum balance in your account.

Some banks even have school savings programs. Kids can open a savings account at school with permission from a parent. They bring their passbook and deposit to school on certain days, when a bank employee visits. That way you can do your banking at school or at the bank and watch your savings grow.

MONEY Makers W. C. Fields was a comedian, writer, director, and movie star. He started his career on the stage. But he became famous in films during the 1920s. The story goes that he opened bank accounts everywhere he went. He liked to use made-up names like Mahatma Kane Jeeves and Otis Criblecoblis. It is thought that he had about seven hundred bank accounts when he died, but not many of them were ever found.

Even More Ways to Save

Banks offer special savings accounts called certificate of deposit accounts (CDs). They pay more interest than a regular savings account. That's because the money must stay in the CD account for a certain length of time—maybe a month, a year, or three years. CDs are a good way for people to save if they won't need to use their money for a long time.

Money market accounts offer another way to save. But money markets might require a higher minimum balance than a regular savings account. They also pay higher interest than a regular savings account. The more money in the account, the higher the interest you will earn.

Another way to save for the future is with an individual retirement account (IRA). IRAs are savings accounts for when you will retire. When you retire, you can take your money out of your IRA.

Chapter 4
Check This Out!

Someday you may be getting a job or going to college. At that time, you may decide to open a checking account. It allows you to spend your money without using cash or going to the bank. You will most likely have to be eighteen years old to open this kind of account.

A check is a promise to pay money to a person or a business. When you pay someone with a check, the exact amount of money you write on the check will be taken out of your account. The money will be paid to the payee—the person or business whose name you write on the check.

Checklist for Check Writing

When you open a checking account, your bank will order checks just for you. They will be printed with:

√ Your name and address

√ Your account number and bank routing number

√ Check numbers

Checks have spaces for you to fill in when you use them:

√ Today's date

√ Name of the person or business you are paying

√ Amount you are paying, written in numbers

√ Amount you are paying, spelled out in words

√ Your signature

√ If you wish, a note telling what you are paying for

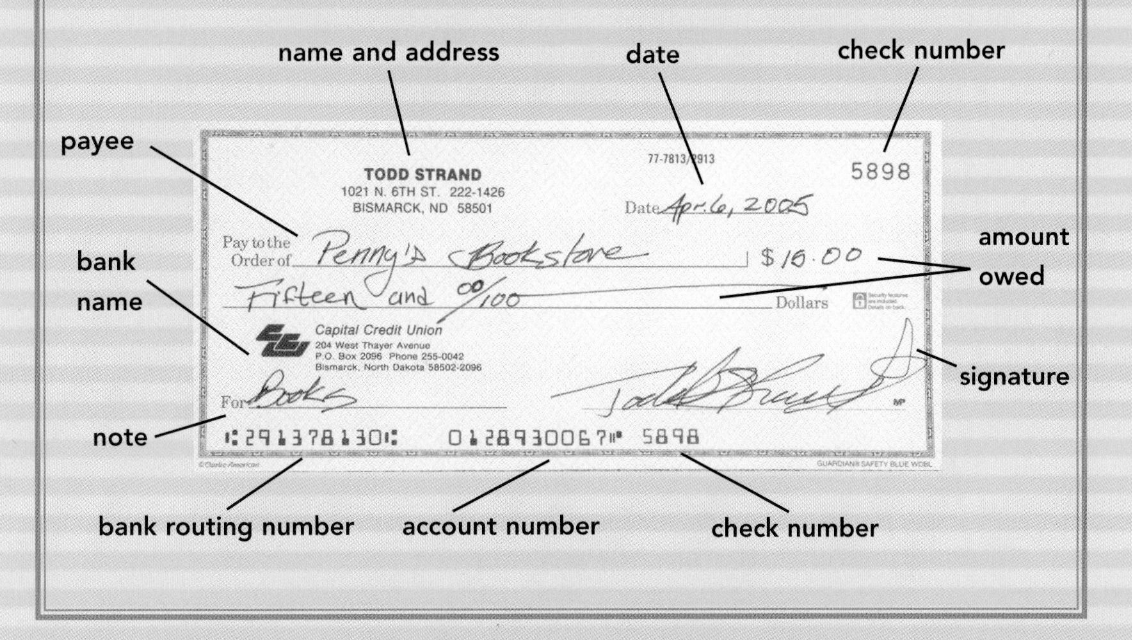

With a checking account, your money remains in a safe place, and it is easy to get at when you need it. A checking account also helps you keep track of the money you spend and of how much you have left.

FUN FACT Could you carry one million dollars? One million dollars in one-dollar bills weighs about forty pounds!

People use checks more often than cash. For one thing, it is easier to carry checks than a lot of cash. It's safer too. A check is only supposed to be cashed by the person or business whose name is written on it. And it is much safer to send a check through the mail than to send cash.

MONEY TALK To cash a check means to exchange it for money at a bank.

What's the Difference?

Checking accounts are different from savings accounts. A regular checking account usually does not pay interest, as a savings account does. But some checking accounts may pay interest if you keep a minimum balance in the account. Banks may also have checking account fees. For example, they may charge for printing checks, for each check written, or for checks that are returned because the account didn't have enough money to cover them.

Claire's Treat

One Saturday Uncle John took Ben and Claire to their soccer games. After soccer, they went to lunch at Ruby's Diner. Uncle John said that Claire should treat everyone to lunch because her team won the game. He was only joking. But when the waiter brought the bill for lunch, Uncle John let Claire give his debit card to the waiter—as if she were paying.

What's a debit card? It's a plastic card that looks like a credit card but works like a check. When Uncle John used his debit card, the money he paid for lunch was subtracted, or deducted, from his checking account, just as if he had written a check.

Here's how it worked. The cashier at the diner slid the card through an electronic machine. The machine read the card and contacted the bank's computer to make sure Uncle John had enough money in his checking account to

pay the bill. The bank's computer subtracted the amount of the bill from the balance in Uncle John's account. Then the computer sent it to the bank account of Ruby's Diner. The cashier gave Uncle John a receipt, which he'll have to remember to record in his checking account register.

If Uncle John hadn't had enough money in his account, what would have happened? The bank would not have allowed the exchange. Uncle John would have had to pay for lunch some other way, with cash, for example.

Checking Up on Your Checks

Along with your printed checks, you will receive a check register for your account. The register is a small notebook where you keep track of withdrawals, deposits, and the balance. Always record the amount of every deposit you make, every check you write, and every debit transaction (withdrawal) in the register. Then be sure to calculate the amount of money that remains in your account.

MONEY TALK *To calculate* means to find the total by adding, subtracting, multiplying, or dividing.

Show Me the Money

You don't want to be like Mr. Cash. Mr. Cash didn't bother keeping his checking account register up to date. He thought he knew how much money he had in his account, so he wrote a check to pay Chip's Tree Trimming Service fifty dollars for trimming his trees. The check bounced. This means Mr. Cash's checking account didn't have enough funds (money) to cover the check. So his bank returned the check to Chip's bank. Mr. Cash had to pay an extra charge to the bank for his bounced check. He had to pay fifty dollars in cash to Chip's bank and thirty-five dollars to his bank. He was lucky he didn't have to pay an additional fee to Chip's too. If Mr. Cash did this often, he could have gone to jail. And he's no longer a welcome customer at Chip's Tree Trimming Service.

WHERE DOES A CHECK GO?

Federal Reserve banks are clearinghouses. A clearinghouse is an office where banks send checks and balance accounts. A check is cleared when it passes through the clearinghouse. For example, when a person deposits a check at his or her bank, the bank sends the check to the Federal Reserve. The Fed credits the bank of the person to whom the check was

BANK ON IT The Federal Reserve sorts checks twenty-four hours a day. It processes 15 to 20 billion checks a year!

written. The Fed then subtracts (debits) the same amount from the account of the second bank (the bank of the person who wrote the check).

The process works like this. Hannah and her mother go shopping for a new bike helmet. Hannah picks out a purple one that costs twenty dollars. Hannah's mom writes a check to the Wright Brothers Cycle Shop to pay for it. Hannah wears her new helmet all the way home. Is that the end of the story? Not yet! Here's what happens to the check:

- The Wright Brothers Cycle Shop deposits the check in its account at Dayton Bank.
- Dayton Bank sends the check to a Federal Reserve bank to be cleared.

- The Federal Reserve bank clears the check by adding a twenty dollar credit to the cycle shop's account at Dayton Bank.
- Then the Fed sends the check to Valley Bank, where Hannah's mother has her account.
- Valley Bank pays the Federal Reserve bank twenty dollars from Hannah's mother's account.
- Hannah's mother receives the canceled, or cleared, check with her bank statement at the end of the month. (Some banks only send the statement.) The statement shows that twenty dollars has been subtracted from her account.

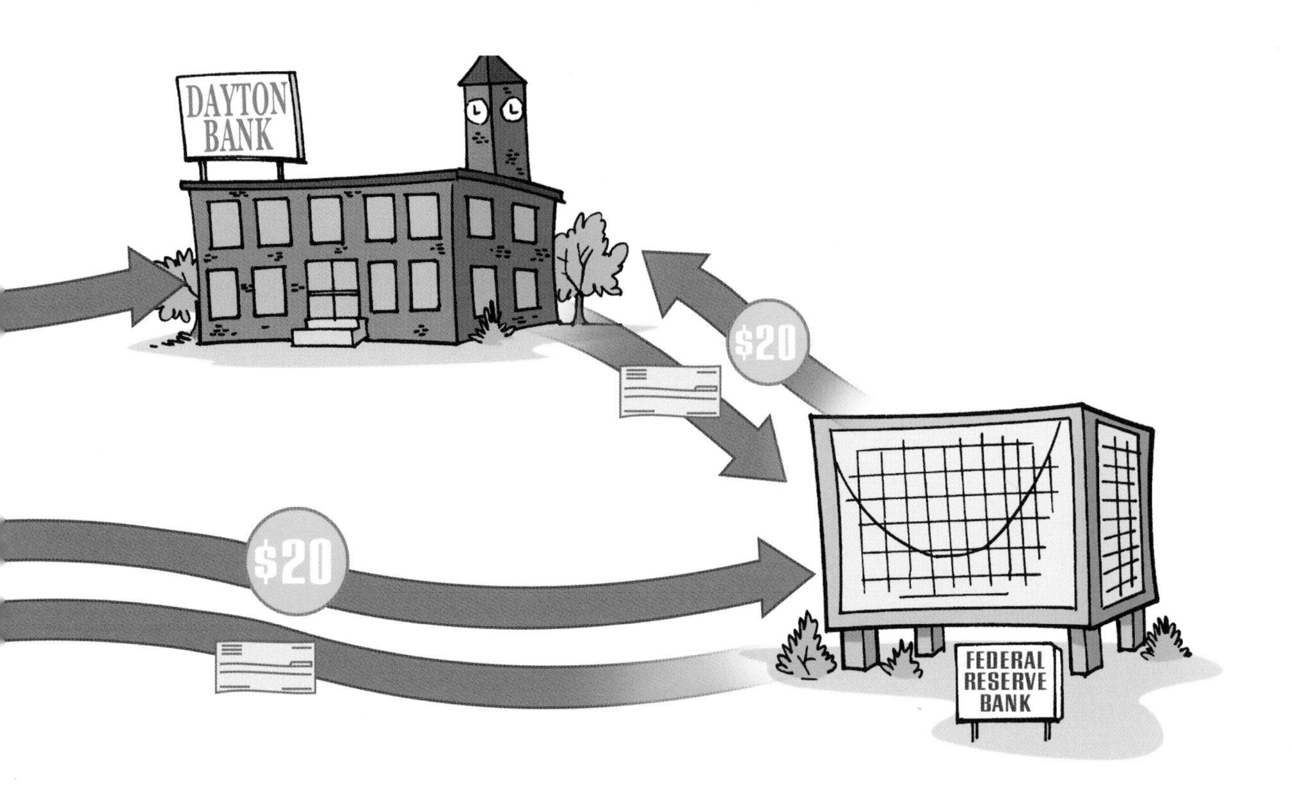

CHAPTER 5
BANKS AT YOUR SERVICE

Banks make loans to people who want to purchase expensive things, such as a car or a house, or to pay for college tuition. Not everyone can get a loan. To receive a loan, you must have a job or be able to prove that you earn money. You must be judged able and likely to repay the money you want to borrow. If you take out a loan from a bank, the bank is giving you credit. The bank believes you intend to pay back the loan. One more thing to know about loans is that they are not free. Remember—banks make money by making loans. You will have to pay the loan back over time and with interest. Loans can usually be paid back in installments—a little at a time, with regular payments.

To take out a loan, a person has to have a good credit report. This is a report that shows whether or not you have a good record of paying what you owe. It tells the name of the institutions or companies that have given credit to you in the past. It also shows whether or not you paid back the credit on time and in full. If your credit is good, you have a good reputation for paying back what you owe.

MONEY TALK Our English word *credit* comes from the Latin word *credo,* which means "I believe." Your credit is good when people believe in your promise and ability to pay back a loan.

A bank employee can help a person understand a credit report and assist with a loan application.

GIVING CREDIT WHERE IT'S DUE

Banks also give credit by issuing credit cards. No doubt you've seen them, but what do you really know about them? They're plastic cards, easy to carry, and easy to use. Most businesses accept credit cards for payment. But that's only part of the story. When you use a credit card, you are buying on credit. This means the bank pays for your purchase, and then you have to pay back the bank. Credit cards are just another kind of loan. Unless you pay the bank in full each month for your credit card purchases, the bank will charge you

BANK ON IT To buy something on credit is to promise to pay later.

Paying for purchases with a credit card is like using borrowed money. Credit card spending should be managed very carefully!

interest (a fee) for the loan. This usually means that the things you buy with a credit card end up being more expensive than if you had paid cash. In fact, the interest on a credit card loan can be much higher than on other types of bank loans. As you can see, credit cards need to be used with care.

Growing Money

Investing is spending money in the hope of making more money. Some people invest in (buy) works of art or antiques. They expect that someday the things they buy will increase in value. Those things can then be sold for more than was paid for them.

A bank can help people invest in stocks or bonds (government certificates). Over time, stocks and bonds can grow in value too. You already know that buying stock is buying a part (or share) of a company. Issuing stock is one way for companies to borrow money. If a company does well, the price of its stock can go up, and investors will earn money. The risk is that stocks could go down. Then investors would lose money. That's why it is wise to learn about a company before investing in it. There is no guarantee that people who invest in stock will make money.

Bonds are certificates issued by the government. When you buy a bond, you are loaning money to the government to help pay for its projects, such as building roads and bridges. You have the government's promise that it will pay you back with interest. Companies also issue bonds. Bonds are purchased for less than their face value (the full

Value Added

The U.S. government first issued savings bonds in 1935. In 1941 President Franklin D. Roosevelt bought the first five-hundred-dollar Series E savings bond. At the beginning of the twenty-first century, about 55 million Americans owned savings bonds.

value printed on them). You hold onto the bond for a fixed period of time. At the end of that time, the bond can be redeemed (exchanged) for its full face value.

Some savings bonds, called U.S. Series EE bonds, can help you earn money tax free for your college education. U.S. Series EE bonds are offered in amounts ranging from fifty dollars to ten thousand dollars. Their purchase price is one-half their face value. That means a one hundred dollar savings bond costs you only fifty dollars. You can cash in this type of bond seventeen years after you buy the bond.

Turn On, Tune In, Pay Up

Computers allow banks to offer many services that make banking easier for people. Instead of getting a paycheck at work, for example, some people choose to have direct deposit. With direct deposit, they do not have to take their paycheck to the bank to cash or deposit it. Instead, their pay is added to their bank account electronically. Their employer sends a computer message to the bank to do this. The bank adds the pay to the worker's account and subtracts it from the employer's account.

Online banking is using a computer and the Internet to connect with your bank's computer. Many banks allow

Many people use online banking to manage their money.

their customers to go online to check their account balances. People might also move some money between their savings account and checking account. Or they might reorder blank checks. Banks allow them to pay their bills online too.

How do bank customers pay their bills online? First, they go to their bank's website. They fill in information (name, address, and telephone number) about the stores or companies to be paid. They also fill in the days they want the bills paid. The bank will contact the companies to find out whether they want to be paid

BANK ON IT A debit is money subtracted from the total in your account.

electronically (by computer) or by check. The bank will automatically send the payments electronically on the days the bank customer has requested.

Carry a Bank Teller with You—An ATM Card

Automated teller machines are called ATMs. Using an ATM, you can make a deposit or withdrawal or check your account balance. You can also move funds from one account to another. You have probably seen ATM machines in airports, in bank lobbies, and in stores and shopping malls. To use an ATM, you need an ATM card. This little plastic card can do the work of a bank teller for you at any time of day or night. To use an ATM card, you must have an account and a special number called a personal identification number (PIN). It is a secret number, and you are the only person who knows it, besides your bank. When you put your card into the ATM, you will need to enter your PIN number by pressing the number keys on the machine. If the

Many banks issue ATM cards with new checking or savings accounts.

PIN number is incorrect, the ATM will not do the banking operation. When the PIN number is correct, you can go ahead and do your banking. The ATM will print a receipt. Keep it so you can write down the amount of your deposit or withdrawal in your check register.

SAFE DEPOSIT BOXES

You already know that a bank vault is a safe place to keep your money. Did you know it is also a place to keep valuables, such as jewelry, coins, stamp collections, and important papers? A safe deposit box is a metal box that is stored in the bank's vault. The boxes come in different sizes. People can rent them to lock their valuables inside. Let's say you keep your stamp collection in your safe deposit box, and you want to look at it. It takes two keys

to unlock the box—yours and the bank's. You must show a bank official your identification and sign a form. The bank official signs the form too and writes down the time. The official takes you to a small, private room and goes to the vault to get your box. He or she brings the box to you and leaves. You unlock it with your key. When you are done, you lock the box and return it to the bank official, who writes down the time you finished. Then the bank official returns the box to the vault.

BANKING JOURNEY

In this book, we journeyed through time from the early days of America to the tweny-first century. Our journey began in the days when Americans had to use English coins to buy something or trade goods. These days millions of paper notes and checks change hands every day, and computers trade money electronically in the blink of an eye.

Many things have changed about the ways in which people go about the business of banking. People's needs for banking services have grown. In turn, banks have continued to expand their services. It's hard to believe that banking will change even more, but it will. Can you imagine how?

Glossary

accounts: arrangements, such as a savings account or a checking account, to keep money in a bank

balance: the amount of money that remains in an account after deposits and withdrawals are made

bank: a place of business for keeping and lending money. Many banks offer other services, such as issuing credit, ATM (automated teller machine) and debit cards, online banking, safe deposit boxes, and investments.

checks: written orders telling a bank to give a certain amount of money to the person or business named on the checks

credit: trust that a person will pay later. A bank gives credit through many kinds of loans.

deposit: money put into an account

interest: money paid to a person or bank for the use of money. For example, people pay interest to a bank for loaning them money. A bank pays people interest for keeping their money in the bank so the bank can use it.

teller: a bank employee who helps people make deposits and withdrawals from their accounts or to transfer money from one account to another

withdrawal: money taken out of an account

Bibliography

Books

Adams, James Ring. *The Big Fix: Inside the S&L Scandal.* New York: John Wiley & Sons, Inc., 1990.

Becker, Thomas W. *The Coin Makers: The Development of Coinage from Earliest Times.* Garden City, NY: Doubleday & Company, Inc., 1969.

Bodnar, Janet. *Dollars & Sense for Kids: What They Need to Know about Money and How to Tell Them.* Washington, DC: The Kiplinger Washington Editors, Inc., 1999.

———. *Money-Smart Kids (and Parents, Too!).* Hyattsville, MD: Kiplinger Books, 1993.

Bungum, Jane E. *Money and Financial Institutions.* Minneapolis: Lerner Publications Company, 1991.

Dunkling, Leslie, and Adrian Room. *The Guinness Book of Money.* New York: Facts on File, 1990.

Dunnan, Nancy. *Banking.* Englewood Cliffs, NJ: Silver Burdett Press, Inc., 1990.

Kennedy, Susan Estabrook. *The Banking Crisis of 1933.* Lexington, KY: University Press of Kentucky, 1973.

Mayer, Martin. *The Fed: The Inside Story of How the World's Most Powerful Financial Institution Drives the Markets.* New York: The Free Press, 2001.

Reinfeld, Fred. *The Story of Civil War Money.* New York: Sterling Publishing Co., Inc., 1959.

Websites

Citizens Bank. "Ownership & History," "Commercial Banking," "Small Business Banking," "Personal Banking." *Citizens Bank.* 2004. http://www.citizensbank.com/aboutus/history/about_ownership.asp. (September 8, 2004). This site provides a history of banking services and an overview of Citizens Bank in Providence, Rhode Island.

Federal Deposit Insurance Corporation (FDIC). *Who Is the FDIC?* July 23, 2003. http://www.fdic.gov/about/learn/symbol/index.html (September 8, 2004). This official site of the FDIC explains how it insures bank deposits.

Federal Reserve Bank of Dallas. "Save and Invest." *Building Wealth: A Beginner's Guide to Securing Your Financial Future.* N. d.

www.dallasfed.org/ca/wealth/3.html (September 7, 2004).
This site presents an overview of saving and investing, including stocks and bonds.

The Federal Reserve Bank of Philadelphia. "The Fed Today." "History of Money and Banking in the United States." "Is the Fed Public or Private?" "The Fed's Role in Making and Setting Monetary Policy." "The Fed Is Protecting Your Money." "The Fed—Helping Keep Banks Safe and Sound." *Economic Education.* N.d. http://www.phil.frb.org/education/ftlesson.html (September 8, 2004).
This site offers lesson plans on various aspects of the Fed as well as a Federal Reserve System map, glossary, and additional Fed websites.

Federal Reserve Bank of Richmond. "Money Museum." *Federal Reserve Bank of Richmond.* N.d. http://www.rich.frb.org/generalinfo/visitors/richmond.html (September 8, 2004).
This site offers a virtual tour of the Money Museum of the Richmond Federal Reserve Bank which tells the story of money in colonial America and the United States.

Federal Reserve Bank of Saint Louis. "In Plain English: Making Sense of the Federal Reserve." *About the Fed.* N.d. http://www.stls.frb.org (September 8, 2004).
This site provides a handy guide to the structure and functions of the Federal Reserve System.

Fidelity Homestead Association. "The History and Purpose of the Savings and Loan Industry." *Fidelity History.* 2000. http://www.fidelityhomestead.com/history.html (September 8, 2004).
This site offers a brief explanation of the history and purpose of the savings and loan industry.

Financial Institutions Division, Ohio Department of Commerce. "Savings and Loans History and Overview." N.d. http://www.com.state.oh.us/ODOC/dfi/slsbhist.htm
This site gives a short history of savings and loan institutions.

Microsoft Corporation. "9 Tips for Raising Money-Smart Children." *msn.Money.* 2004. http://www.moneycentral.msn.com/articles/family/basics/8511.asp (September 8, 2004).
The site offers tips for helping kids learn about managing money.

Savings Bank of Walpole. "What Is a Mutual Savings Bank?" *Savings Bank of Walpole.* 2003. http://www.walpolebank.com/mutual.htm (September 8, 2004).
This site gives a brief history of mutual savings banks.

U.S. Department of Health, Education, and Welfare, Social Security Administration. "Social Security Numbers." "Your Social Security Number and Card." "History and Use of Social Security Numbers." "Social Security Number Chronology." *Social Security Online: History.* N.d. http://www.ssa.gov/history/ssn/ssnpamphlet.html (September 8, 2004).
This is a U.S. government site with information on the history and use of Social Security numbers.

U.S. Department of the Treasury. *The Bureau of Engraving and Printing.* N.d. http://www.bep.treas.gov. (September 7, 2004).
This site contains information on U.S. bank notes and other money facts.

U.S. Department of the Treasury. "Currency and Coins." "Distribution of Currency & Coins." "Duties & Functions." "History of the Treasury." "For Kids." N.d. http://www.ustreas.gov/education/fact-sheets/currency/index.html (September 8, 2004).
This U.S. Treasury site describes how Federal Reserve banks distribute money. It also has a special site with related interactive government links for kids.

Further Reading and Websites

Books

Arnold, Oren. *Marvels of the U.S. Mint.* New York: Abelard-Schuman, 1972.

Cribb, Joe. *Eyewitness: Money.* New York: DK Publishing, Inc., 2000.

Drobot, Eve. *Money.* New York: Prentice Hall Books for Young Readers, 1987.

Giesecke, Ernestine. *Everyday Banking: Consumer Banking.* Chicago: Heinemann Library, 2002.

———. *Money Business: Banks and Banking.* Chicago: Heinemann Library, 2002.

Godfrey, Neale S. *Ultimate Kids' Money Book.* New York: Simon & Schuster Books for Young Readers, 1998.

Mayr, Diane. *The Everything Kids' Money Book.* Avon, MA: Adams Media Corporation, 2000.

Schwartz, David M. *If You Made a Million.* New York: William Morrow & Co., 1994.

Sirimarco, Elizabeth. *At the Bank.* Chanhassen, MN: Child's World, Inc., 1999.

Video and DVD

Piggy Banks to Money Markets: A Video Guide to Dollars & Sense." South Bend, IN: Peter Pan, 2002. This video/DVD covers subjects such as what money is, how people get money, what people do with money, and making choices.

Websites

h.i.p. Pocket Change
http://www.usmint.gov/kids/flashIndex.cfm
This U.S. Mint website features learning games for kids, as well as plans, guides, and ideas for teachers.

KidsBank.com
http://www.kidsbank.com/
Sovereign Bank, 2004. A fun place for kids to learn about money and banking.

Money Central Station
http://www.moneyfactory.com/kids/start.html
This is an interactive U.S. Treasury site where kids can play games to learn about money.

Money Museum, Federal Reserve Bank of Richmond
http://www.rich.frb.org/research/econed/museum/
A virtual tour of the Fifth District Money Museum with exhibits of trade in colonial America and of the First Bank of the United States. This site also features an audio tour.

The U.S. Department of the Treasury
http://www.treas.gov/kids/
The U.S. Department of the Treasury site offers links to government websites designed especially for kids, including the U.S. Mint, the Bureau of Engraving and Printing, and U.S. savings bonds.

Sights to Visit

The Denver Mint

United States Mint
Tour Information
320 West Colfax Avenue
Denver, CO 80204-2693
(303) 405-4766
The U.S. Mint needs two week's notice for tours, where visitors will see how coins are made.

The Philadelphia Mint

United States Mint
Tour Information
151 North Independence Mall East
Philadelphia, PA 19106-1886
(215) 408-0114
The U.S. Mint needs two week's notice for tours, where visitors will see how coins are made.

United States Treasury Building

Fifteenth and Pennsylvania Avenue, NW
Washington, DC
http://www.treas.gov/education/tour/index.html
The main treasury building is the third-oldest building in Washington, D.C., and dates from 1836.

Your Area's Federal Reserve Bank

http://www.federalreserve.gov/fraddress.htm
Federal Reserve banks are located in Atlanta, Georgia; Boston, Massachusetts; Chicago, Illinois; Cleveland, Ohio; Dallas, Texas; Kansas City, Missouri; Minneapolis, Minnesota; New York, New York; Philadelphia, Pennsylvania; Richmond, Virginia; San Francisco, California; and Saint Louis, Missouri.

Your Local Bank

Use a phone book or the Internet to find banks in your area. Call to inquire about tours. Many banks enjoy showing kids around.

INDEX

About the Author

Barbara Allman writes for children and teachers. She is the author of *Musical Genius—A Story about Wolfgang Amadeus Mozart; Dance of the Swan—A Story about Anna Pavlova;* and *Her Piano Sang—A Story about Clara Schumann.* She lives in Jacksonville, Oregon.

Photo Acknowledgments

Bill Hauser, pp. 3, 4, 12, 16, 18, 21, 24, 27, 29, 30–31, 32, 39; Courtesy Trustees of the British Museum, p. 5 (top); Hypnoclips, pp. 5 (bottom), 7, 9, 14 (both), 26, 28, 29, 33 (top), 34 (top), 37 (bottom); © Bettmann/CORBIS, p. 10; Brand X Pictures, pp. 20, 38; © Todd Strand/Independent Picture Service, p. 25; © SuperStock Inc./SuperStock, p. 33 (bottom); © Anton Vengo/SuperStock, p. 34 (bottom); © Jon Feingersh/CORBIS, p. 37 (top).

Front cover: Bill Hauser. Back cover: Hypnoclips (both).